Destiny Decisions

Camille Sylvester

BookLeaf Publishing

India | USA | UK

Presentation by *BookLeaf Publishing*

Web: www.bookleafpub.com

E-mail: info@bookleafpub.com

ISBN: 978-93-5744-749-2

First edition 2022

DEDICATION

I dedicate this book, my first published work to God. I have been very blessed though his love and favor.

ACKNOWLEDGEMENT

I would like to acknowledge my mom and dad, they have taught me so many things over the years. I would like to acknowledge my friends who continue to share their lives and experiences with me

PREFACE

I have always loved books. I used to write poetry as a child and as I got older I stopped. I'm taking this opportunity to write my experiences, the good, bad and ugly.

Promises

What is a promise?
A sweet agreement between oneself or with
another
Today I made a promise
A promise to honour my God
A promise to honour my purpose
A promise to put myself first
A promise to make my parents and family proud
A promise to be the best in everything I do
A promise to have the right man cover me in
love
A promise to enjoy each day I have been given
My promises I hope to keep

Killing me Softly

I want to thank the man who has helped me
become the woman I am
He wore different faces, came with different
names but had the same motive
Killing me softly

Slowly, gently, with unnerving kindness and
then would attack me in the most vicious ways
Strike me in the heart (the seat of the soul)
Killing me softly

He would make promises and I ate them like
candy
He would utter sweet words but his actions were
like swords
Killing me softly

Thank you for the lessons
I am now breaking the cycle
Healing from toxic words and lies covered in
emotion
I will no longer be killed softly

Drowning in your love

I'm drowning in your love
I'm drowning in your love
Where would I be?
What would I do, without you?

I'm drowning in your love
I'm drowning in your love

Thank you for all you do
Glory to the one most High God

My Future Babies Are Coming

My future babies are coming
My future babies are coming
I can't wait to meet you
I can't wait to hold you

My future babies are coming
My future babies are coming

I can't wait to teach
I can't wait to learn from you

My future babies are coming
My future babies are coming

A Year of Untapped Greatness

As a child I had big dreams
I knew I was born to do great things
But as grew older, I learned to do small things
I prioritized other people's needs above my own

As an adult I had small dreams
I forgot what I was born to do
As time went by, I relearned to do great things
I prioritized my needs above other people

I challenged myself to a year of greatness
I challenged myself to do be better each day
I challenged myself to speak love and favour
over me

All I need is a year
A year of untapped greatness
Who will I become?
What will I learn?
What great things will I accomplish?

Touched by You

I am touched by you
I am touched by you
I am touched by you

My God, my everything

I am touched by you
I am touched by you
I am touched by you

Thank you for what you've given me
Thank you for your tender mercies
Thank you for your patient ways

They are priceless
They're appreciated

I am touched by you
I am touched by you
I am touched by you

Fire & Ice

I got that fire and I got that ice
I got that fire and I got that ice

I wear the crown
I gear the sensor
I hold the scepter

You're not around to keep me down
You're not here to tear me down

I got that fire and I got that ice
I got that fire and I got that ice

I'm wide awake now to unleash my voice
I'm gaining victory all around town

To the Woman I'm Becoming

To the Woman I'm Becoming
I'm excited to meet you
I'm excited to see the things you're going to do
I'm excited to hear if your new adventures
I'm excited to experience what you have to offer

To the Woman I'm Becoming
Be Focused
Be Strong
Be Courageous

To the Woman I'm Becoming
Love yourself
Love others
Love Life, it's a beautiful thing

To the Woman I'm Becoming
I'm excited to meet you
I'm excited to see the things you're going to do
I'm excited to hear of your new adventures
I'm excited to experience what you have to offer

Gratitude

Gratitude

A small word but has a big impact
A small word but means the world to the
recipient
A small word but can shift atmospheres

What are you grateful for?
Who are you grateful for?
When are you in a grateful mood?
Where are you the most grateful?

Small questions but can lead to big results
Small questions but can transform your mind
Small questions but can lead a lifestyle of peace

Gratitude

Music to my ears

Vibration... Frequency...Sound
They all have one thing in common energy
Energy which has the power to shift emotions
Emotions which have the power to change
actions
Actions which have the power to change destiny

Destiny is like having a long awaited gift
A gift when received is like music
Music to my ears
My ears which receive the sounds of joy

Your Grace

Your Grace sustains
Your Grace abounds
Your Grace heals
Your Grace uplifts

Your Grace is One of a Kind
Your Grace is all I need
Your Grace covers me
Your Grace surrounds me

Thank you Lord for Your Grace

I Can't Live Without You

My God, My God
I can't live without you
My God, My God
I can't live without you

Where would I be without you?
Where would I go without you?
How can I live without you?

My God, My God
I can't live without you
My God, My God
I can't live without you

Thank you for being in my life
Thank you for being my light
Thank you for all you do, in everything you do

My God, My God
I can't live without you
My God, My God
I can't live without you

Fighting my battles

I am weak
I am broken
I am tired

In life, some things come for your mind
Others come for your body
The most deadly come for your soul

I am weak
I am broken
I am tired

God is fighting my battles
The God who lives, loves and sees
My God whose protection I am under
God is fighting my battles
Both the seen and unseen

The Winds of the Season

Every season is magical
Every season is valuable
Every season has its purpose

In a new season, focus your energy
On the lessons and blessings
When in season

Some seasons are sad
Some seasons are mad
Some seasons are glad

Regardless of the winds of the season
Always remember there is a purpose
A purpose which can't always been explained
But purpose which is felt and must be actualized

Profound Wisdom

What is wisdom?
Why do we need wisdom?
How do we apply wisdom?

Wisdom the ability to discern what is right
Wisdom enhances your life
Wisdom prepares you for opportunities

The fear of God is the beginning of wisdom
Wisdom prolongs life
Wisdom brings wealth

Profound wisdom is needed in life
To acquire hidden treasures and resources

Profound wisdom is needed in life
To build relationships

Profound wisdom is needed in life
To bring quality and peace

Proud wisdom is needed in life

Higher Ground

Lord take me to a higher ground
A higher realm
A higher sound

I need your word more than ever
I seek your counsel in hidden places
I hear the sound of your voice

Lord take me to a higher ground
Transformation of my mind
Restoration of my heart
Elevation of my soul

Lord take me to a higher ground

Only In Your Prescence

Only in your presence do I seek
Only in your presence do I hear
Only in your presence do I move

In the presence of others I guard my heart
In the presence of others I still my tongue
In the presence of others hold my peace

Only in your presence do I seek
Only in your presence do I hear
Only in your presence do I move

Power of Prayer

Prayers are real
Prayers are powerful
Prayers are magical

There are days when you are weak with sorrow
There are days when you are full of joy

No matter the day
Learn to pray
Learn to be thankful
Learn to count your blessings

Prayer is direct communion with God
He can give insight and knowledge
He may give a warning and turns events
He may be silent

Prayers are real
Prayers are powerful
Prayers are magical

Have you prayed today?

Princess and Baby

Princess and Baby
My second and third pets
Cheddar was the first, who ran away in a fright

Two baby kittens who stayed together
Out of a litter of eight

After fifteen years
You're both family
I was with you for your first days of life
I will be with you in your last days of life

Princess and Baby
The sweetest cats you'll ever meet

Trees

They tell a lifetime of stories
They tell a history of knowledge
They tell their own story

They stand firm
They stand their ground
They may sway to and fro in the wind

They adapt to their environments
They change in different seasons
Some may grow fruit and nuts

Learn to listen to the trees
Observe their hidden wisdom
Be strong and fruitful as a tree

True Love

True love is pure
True love is kind
True love is patient

To my husband to come
My God appointed husband

Will you show me true love?
Do you promise to love me in sickness and
health?
Do you swear to honour our vows and bring
glory to our God?

True love protects
True love hopes
True love never fails

www.ingramcontent.com/pod-product-compliance
Lightning Source LLC
LaVergne TN
LVHW021348200726
843509LV00014B/2724